KARATE WARRIOR

KARATE WARRIOR

A BEGINNER'S GUIDE TO MARTIAL ARTS

AUSTIN ST. JOHN

WITH STEVE ROWE

COURAGE BOOKS

A PROMOTIONAL REPRINT COMPANY BOOK
© 1996 by Revelations Films, Ltd.

First published in the United States in 1996 by Running Press Book Publishers

Printed in China

9 8 7 6 5 4 3 2 1
Digit on the right indicates the number of this printing

Library of Congress Cataloging-in-Publication Number 96-68388

ISBN 1-56138-784-3

This book may be ordered by mail from the publisher. Please include $2.50 for postage and handling. *But try your bookstore first!*

Running Press Book Publishers
125 South Twenty-second Street
Philadelphia, Pennsylvania 19103-4399

9.99

Contents

INTRODUCTION

Hi! Those of you who have watched me in The Mighty Morphin Power Rangers *TV show as Jason, the Red Ranger, will know how important the martial arts are to me – not just in terms of physical training but as a philosophy for life.*

Now I am inviting all of you to join me on an exciting journey through those arts. I'll be giving you as much advice as possible along the way, aided by photographs taken during my recent visit to England. I'll also be revealing some of the secrets and skills which enabled me to become a Power Ranger, but I want to make it clear from the start that this is only a brief introduction to the mysteries of the martial arts. You are not going to become experts overnight! It takes years of training and practice.

I admit the photographs here look pretty exciting, but please don't try anything too ambitious or dangerous yourselves. This book is meant as an introductory guide only. The best advice I can give you is that if you're interested, join a recognized club where you can receive qualified instruction.

So be careful. To keep safe, play safe!

Austin St. John

You
Can Be a
Karate
Warrior

You Can Be a Karate Warrior

The Power Rangers were created to make the world a better place in which to live. That, I'm proud to say, has been my main achievement as one of their members.

The martial arts were devised centuries ago to achieve exactly the same goal: to make the world a better place – and to make you a better person.

The martial arts are as old as mankind itself. Peace has always been maintained by learning how to deal with anger, violence and fear – not just in other people, but within ourselves as well. Through the mental disciplines of the martial arts you will discover the secret behind being peaceful and calm, and extending that peace to those around you. You will also learn the physical skills and techniques used to counter any violence found in others.

Plus, the martial arts are fun to practice and a good way of keeping fit!

In the following pages I will discuss the history of these ancient and noble Arts. I'll start by recalling

the distant past, a time of
warrior kings, princes and, of
course, princesses! Together
we will explore the origins of
the martial arts and learn
how to approach their
philosophy and training.

Later I will show you how
to use your body properly,
including basic techniques
and correct exercises. I will
discuss all the basic principles
of training and combat,
explaining why, when and
how you should put them
into practice. Some great
photographs are used to
make these vital points even
clearer.

I will give you some very
important safety hints and

pass on the secrets to warming up and cooling down correctly. I will also give you tips on how to find a good club and instructor.

Toward the end of the book you'll see photographs of some of my favorite routines and techniques. These more advanced moves should only be attempted by a martial artist with many years of training and practice. I will explain how to use what you've learned in your weekly class routines to create more complex moves like those you've seen performed by the Power Rangers.

Never demonstrate your hard-earned skills on the playground.

A martial artist does not show off his own skills in such a way. Only use them at your club, preferably with a mat underneath you. Remember, if you are going to do practice, do it right!

So let me teach you the lessons that every Power Ranger takes to heart. Then you too can become a karate warrior!

HISTORY MYSTERY AND ROMANCE

The ancient origins of the martial arts are lost in the mists of time, but we do know something of their early history. Over 2,500 years ago a prince was born in Kapilavastu, India, just inside present day Nepal. He was the son of the king of the Sakya warriors, and became highly skilled in the arts of fighting and warfare. In his teenage years, however, he underwent a deep spiritual experience and saw the error of his warring ways. He renounced his former life and became a great spiritual leader; a man of profound wisdom, penetrating vision and great compassion.

The prince left his father's court to follow a spiritual path. His teachings spread throughout China, Korea and Japan. He became known as the Buddha and wherever he went, he influenced the beliefs of those who listened to him preach. He convinced people that they should live peacefully and that warfare should be avoided. Bearing this in mind, the people who believed in Buddha's message of peace developed their fighting skills non-agressively, learning to use an attacker's energy against him. This is still the governing principle of many of the martial arts today –

the deflection of an enemy's energy.

If you choose to study a formal discipline of the martial arts you will soon realize how heavily they are influenced by religion and philosophy. A great deal of Eastern culture revolves around Buddhism (the followers of Buddha). The "do" in karatedo, judo, aikido, kendo, tae kwon do and others literally means "the way," reflecting Buddha's teachings about "the way" of peace and "the way" of life. You may find that many of the words and phrases used in our modern martial arts seem a little strange, but this is because they have their roots in the ancient cultures and languages of the Far East.

In the sixth century, Boddidharma, an Indian priest, visited the Shaolin temple in China where he preached Zen Buddhism, a variation on the teachings of Buddha. Boddidharma also gave instruction in eighteen self-defense exercises known as Shaolin Eighteen Monk Boxing. This martial art spread throughout China with each new teacher developing and refining the skills he passed on. By the time the exercises reached Korea and Japan, they had become what we would recognize today as a form of kung fu. All Western forms of the martial arts can be traced back to the ancient Shaolin Eighteen Monk Boxing techniques.

The martial arts are now practiced worldwide for a variety of reasons; as a means of self-defense and law enforcement, in competitive sports, and as exercise to improve physical fitness. Most disciplines are initially graded into different color belts leading up to the coveted black belt or black sash. Once the black belt has been achieved, the grades advance further in degrees or "dan" grades. A first dan is a beginner black belt, while a fifth dan is usually acknowledged as a master. The highest grade, which

only few achieve, is the tenth dan. I started my martial arts training when I was very young. I was taught at first by my father but have since studied thirteen different martial arts and have black belt dans in four of them.

I credit my kicking skills to the Korean disciplines, my hand techniques to the Japanese and my grappling talents to the Chinese. The martial arts are certainly a healthy mix of cultures!

When my father – who

was a martial arts instructor – was teaching me the basic skills, he told me many enchanting stories from oriental mythology about dragons. As the dragon is such an important symbol in the East, I have adopted a dragon emblem for my system of training. My pupils proudly wear an embroidered dragon on their martial arts clothing.

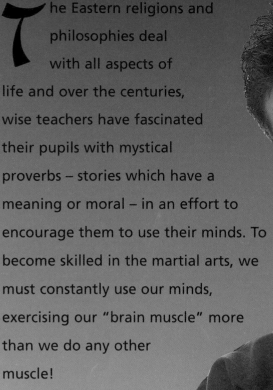

The Eastern religions and philosophies deal with all aspects of life and over the centuries, wise teachers have fascinated their pupils with mystical proverbs – stories which have a meaning or moral – in an effort to encourage them to use their minds. To become skilled in the martial arts, we must constantly use our minds, exercising our "brain muscle" more than we do any other muscle!

This doesn't simply mean thinking about how to kick higher, punch harder or leap further. We must also try to improve our general outlook, our social skills and our concentration. All of these things combine to help create our personalities and, in improving these character traits, we can build confidence and create the right state of mind to encourage further growth and development on all fronts. To get better, you have to try harder!

Attitude, Outlook and Effort

Attitude

A martial artist should constantly be aware of his or her state of mind. If we allow ourselves to adopt a negative attitude, then even the smallest of tasks can seem as impossible as moving a mountain. A negative point of view colors our interpretation of what we feel is "right" and "normal." We must always strive to maintain a positive attitude. This generates optimism, helping us to see that our goals are achievable, to think our way around problems, and to improve our martial arts techniques. With a positive attitude, you can figure out how to move that mountain.

Outlook

Everything we say and everything we do affects those around us. A single word or phrase can deeply wound or, alternatively, make a person extremely happy. The power of speech is immensely strong and can do more harm than all the physical movements of the martial arts put together. There is an old Chinese proverb that states: "Think three times before you speak and only then, if you think it is still worth saying, give it voice." If we think before we speak, we can avoid upsetting those around us. In avoiding upsetting people, we can also avoid conflict. Consideration for others is an excellent form of self-defense!

Showing kindness to others helps us to stay calm, stay cool and stay in control of our own behavior. Thoughtful behavior is the mark of the true martial arts enthusiast.

EFFORT

We must put enthusiastic effort into all the things we do; whether it be keeping up our martial arts training or doing homework on time. If we put too little effort into the things we do, we will never reach our goals. It is important to realize how much work we need to do to achieve any target we set for ourselves. A sudden spurt of activity rarely brings results. Higher standards in whatever we do can always be achieved through steady, consistent effort over a sensible period of time. This is most definitely true of martial arts training.

We must always try to organize our thoughts in a disciplined manner. Concentration is essential in martial arts in order to avoid injuring yourself, to prevent an opponent from gaining the upper hand and to help deliver power and accuracy in your moves. You cannot concentrate, of course, with a jumble of thoughts milling around in your head. Think of organizing your thoughts just like saving and closing files on your computer. The extra space gives you more capacity for the work at hand, more capacity being greater concentration. Organization, discipline and concentration are indispensible tools for the martial artist, but it takes a great deal of sustained effort to bring these tools within reach.

HOW TO LEARN THE MARTIAL ARTS

I feel that it's very important for anyone who wants to learn one of the martial arts disciplines to do so in a correct and safe manner. The best way to do this is to join a proper club specializing in your chosen martial art. Even then, however, you must be happy with the club and the instruction you receive in order to make good progress in learning your techniques. I would urge every newcomer to follow the simple guidlines listed below.

1 No matter how good the instructor tells you his club is, do not join if the club is not affiliated to the relevant governing body.

2 Make sure that your club has personal accident insurance and member-to-member liability for each of its students and that your registration form lists pertinent medical information and a contact person in the event of an accident.

(see page 34) and pre-arranged pairs work. Children under the age of twelve should not fight at all, while twelve- to sixteen-year-olds should only "spar" under the eye of a trained instructor.

3 Notify the instructor if you have a health condition such as asthma or diabetes.

4 Although training should include an element of mental discipline, if you feel you are being bullied or are being forced to do things you do not want to do, leave the club. Likewise, if your club is only interested in winning competitions and is not interested in the well-being of the individual students, you should find another club.

5 Make sure you are being trained with others of your own age. It's impossible to train adults and children together as their body structure, requirements and weight are so different.

6 Training should concentrate on teaching good manners and strong, basic techniques as well as *kata*

7 Check all the fees before you enroll. You will usually have to pay registration, training and equipment fees before you begin, but you may then be asked to pay annual registration, grading and training fees as you progress. Make sure you know what all the various charges are – and that there are no hidden extras.

WHAT TO WEAR

According to which martial art discipline you decide to start with, you will have to get the appropriate clothing. It is usual to purchase the *karategi* and *judogi* through your instructor. These items resemble old oriental peasant clothing, consisting of loose-fitting drawstring pants and a wrap-over jacket. The clothes come in various thicknesses of cloth, depending on the type of activity you are planning to undertake.

When you buy your clothes, be aware of the possibility of shrinkage. Buy the best you can afford because if you train hard, these outfits can wear out quite quickly! Although they come in many colors, it is traditional to wear white. A club logo is usually worn over the left breast and normally reflects the character of the club – like the dragon on my suits.

The belt (or *obi* in Japanese) is wound around the waist twice, with a double thickness at the back to support the spine. It is then tied in a kind of reef knot at the front. These colored cotton belts let the instructor know which techniques to teach you in class and are therefore an indication of your progress. Once you have achieved a black belt, you will find it is made from white cotton covered in black silk. The black silk will gradually wear off,

revealing the white cotton underneath, and reminding the expert of his or her humble beginnings. After all, we are all students for life, constantly learning new things. Remember, the better you get, the more humble you should become.

The way you look after your clothes is a reflection of your character. They should be simple, clean and kept in a good state of repair. Every time you put on your suit, you should renew your commitment to do your best in each session.

HEALTH

Let's briefly look at health for a moment, as good body maintenance is essential to us all. Obviously, a healthy body and a healthy mind are important not just for martial arts training but for a happy life as well. To achieve a healthy body and mind it's vital to do some form of physical activity at least three times a week for at least twenty minutes at a time. Preferably you should do some exercise every day.

Good, natural, deep breathing is a fine way of staying relaxed, ensuring that enough oxygen gets into your bloodstream. Try breathing in by pushing your lower abdomen out. When you have completed your incoming breath, press your abdominal muscles in for a count of three and then slowly release your breath. Repeat the process. This is the natural breathing rhythm.

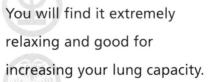

You will find it extremely relaxing and good for increasing your lung capacity.

Good posture is also important because it allows our bodies to function in the most effective manner. A lot of unnecessary tension comes from our back muscles fighting to keep our bodies upright because we have a natural tendency to slouch. From a combatant's point of view, it is very easy to unbalance someone who is already struggling to stay upright!

If you stand and sit incorrectly you end up squashing your stomach, kidneys, spleen and the other organs so that they are unable to perform their duties efficiently. You may then suffer from discomfort and ill-health. Remember, prevention is better than cure so make an effort and learn to sit and stand with a straight back.

TRAINING

When you train, it is important to warm up and later cool down properly. This prevents injuries to your muscles, tendons and joints. When you first start training in your chosen martial art, the warming up and cooling down exercises are the first things that you are taught. As you become more skillful, you can use the basic techniques to warm up, and then move on to the more complex maneuvers as your muscles loosen up.

It is best to start by increasing the heart rate with small movements, like jogging in place or skipping, until you get a light sweat or sheen on your skin. Your body is now prepared to increase the range of movements. Martial arts training consists of a diverse range of movements in all directions, so your body really requires a proper warm up before you start learning various *kata* and techniques.

Austin's Warm Up & Cool Down

1
Traditional
"Horse Stance"

2
Right leg raise

3
Left leg raise

4
Body twist
to left

5
Body twist
to right

6
Close chest,
open shoulders

7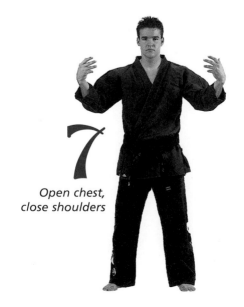
Open chest,
close shoulders

8
Turn head
to left

9
Turn head
to right

I usually start with a short period of meditation to prepare my mind for the training session and help my concentration.

I then perform exercises that increase my heart and breathing rates. Once I'm gently sweating, I move into the "deep muscle" warm up, which differs according to the training session I'm about to do. After this I practice the most simple techniques, building in complexity as I progress.

When I have finished the main part of my training, I return to the less complex techniques to cool down. I find that deep stretching is a good way to relax the body. I finish with another short period of meditation to prepare myself for the outside world again.

A good way to look at your training session is to see half of it as the warm up and the other half as the cool down.

Remember that I have been training for many years, so my exercise routines will be very different from those of a beginner. Don't just copy the photographs in this book but get expert advise and tuition.

10
Bend over hamstring stretch with legs bent

11
Concentrating on left leg stretch

12
Concentrating on right leg stretch

13

Lunge stretch
(should be
performed on
both sides)

14

Crouch stretch
to right

15

Crouch stretch
to left

16

Front splits
to left

17

Front splits
to right

Seated "Knee Wings"

18

19

Seated
hamstring
stretch

20

Concentrated hamstring stretch on
one side (should be
performed on
both sides)

NUTRITION

There are three basic food groups which our bodies require to maintain good health: proteins, carbohydrates and fats. Vitamins and minerals are also important in a healthy, balanced diet.

Proteins are the building blocks of the body. Without them you will not make any significant gains in strength, no matter how hard you train. Foods rich in protein are eggs, milk, fish, chicken and red meat. Milk is especially good for you because it contains calcium, which strengthens your bones and teeth.

Carbohydrates come in two forms, simple and complex. Simple carbohydrates enter the bloodstream quickly and give instant energy. This is why your body sometimes craves a bar of chocolate after you've been training. You need a sugar rush to help your body cope with the excess of energy that's been spent. The effects of simple carbohydrates do not last long. Complex carbohydrates act more slowly on the body, providing a much longer lasting source of energy. Complex carbohydrates are found in starchy food like potatoes, brown rice, bread and pasta.

Fats and oils can be obtained from a variety of animal and vegetable sources. A certain amount in your diet is important, but be careful not to have too much – fat is loaded with calories and once stored on the body, is hard to shift! Try not to use butter when you can use a polyunsaturated margarine, and don't eat too many fried foods. Fresh fruit and vegetables are much better for you, and contain plenty of vitamins and minerals which are essential to a healthy body and clear skin.

To maintain a healthy body, try to avoid table salt and sugar, sweets and cakes. Eat grilled or lightly steamed food whenever possible; if you over-cook vegetables all the vitamins are killed and the food becomes worthless as well as tasting bland. Try to eat small meals often throughout the day, and don't eat just before you go to bed. You are the best judge of how you feel. If you look and feel good, then your eating routine is obviously working!

REST

Sleep is vital for the body. A tired body will not perform as well as a rested one. Eight hours' sleep at night is the recommended amount, but this varies from person to person. Again, go by how you feel and learn to listen to your body. If it's telling you it's exhausted, get more sleep!

As you can see, a combination of the above is essential for your physical and mental well-being. It's important for you to get in touch with both your mind and body. You can do that if you act on the advice given here. Do your own research into what your body requires and start experimenting. You'll feel much better for it!

Confucius said: "A journey of a thousand miles begins with one step." Therefore, when you begin training in your chosen martial art, you should start with simple, basic techniques. These consist of hand strikes, kicks, locks and throws, all performed individually, carefully and slowly. As you increase in confidence your speed in performing these basic maneuvers will also increase.

You never really finish your basic training. Every time you need to improve a technique, whatever grade you are, you always break the movement down by returning to your basic steps. And as I've said already, practicing them is a great way to warm up!

You will move on to performing the basics in sequences of twos and threes. As you master these you will increase your combinations to six or more moves. Combinations are a great way of improving your fighting moves, whether you are training on your own or in a class.

STEP-BY-STEP TO SUCCESS

FORMS

As you begin to feel comfortable with the basics and subsequent combinations, you will begin to train in forms known as *kata.* These are ancient sequences of basic movements designed to pass on the skills of the masters to the novices. These look like fights against multiple attackers but are in fact a condensed catalogue of techniques, strategies and training methods which take

years of top-level instruction to carry out successfully.

Remember that there were no books, instructional videos or television programs when the martial arts were developed. The masters had to pass on their methods of instruction to their novices by other means. This is why they developed the *kata;* forms were a handy way of remembering thousands of strikes, kicks, locks, blocks and throws.

You will normally start with the most simple *kata* and gradually build up to the most complex. Most *kata* use around twenty different movements, but the basic ones consist of only two or three. Well-executed *kata* are said to resemble meditation in motion.

PRE-ARRANGED PAIRS WORK

You will also begin formalized pairs work training. This training is essential for learning awareness, distance, timing, control, body coordination, strategy and etiquette. You will start with the most simple techniques – moving away from an attack and then returning the force.

Your pairs work will then become more complex. You will learn how to move forwards to redirect an attack. You will utilize your partner's incoming energy to strike at vital points on the body and lock or throw the opponent into submission. This is very difficult and requires much skill and control.

Remember that your training partner is there to help you. Remember too that although you train together as opponents you must take great care with one another. If you injure your partner then you defeat the whole object of training, which is learning awareness and yet being mindful of others.

THE TRAINING/GRADING SYLLABUS

All these skills, techniques and strategies are put together in a progressive format called the training or grading syllabus. Your knowledge is tested at gradings, which is how you move on to the next color belt or grade.

The martial arts grading is very formal and structured. It makes for a good learning environment – you always know what you have to learn and what you have to achieve to progress. A good, tried and tested system means the structure is there for you to follow in the footsteps of those who have already made the grade.

Both gradings and competitions are a great way to test your newly-acquired skills. It is easy to perform your techniques in class or at home but you need to test them in a high-pressure situation. Gradings and competitions provide that setting.

There are four basic principles upon which all good martial arts techniques are founded. All techniques are designed to strengthen these principles in the practitioner.

The same principles that make the martial artist strong, will also make his opponent weak. All fighting strategy, therefore, is designed to maintain the practitioner's – and break his opponent's – four by four martial technique.

Over the following pages we talk about the two categories – **Defense** (how to protect yourself from an attack) and **Attack** (how to destroy or break your opponents defense).

4x4

MARTIAL

TECHNIQUE

PRINCIPLE 1: OPPOSITE FORCE THROUGH THE FEET

DEFENSE: All directional power and resistance depends on the pressure of the feet on the floor. Therefore, when you want to direct your power backwards, you must push forwards. Although we are not conscious of it, we have to maintain a constant pressure downwards through our feet just to stand upright. When we are training, whatever technique we are using, the initial power drive will come

from an opposite power drive applied through the feet. The more we study this, the more we will understand the force at our disposal.

ATTACK: The principle of your technique must be designed to destroy your opponent's sense of balance. If he cannot apply pressure with his feet, he will not have the power to drive his own movement or to resist yours. You will then see dramatic results in the application of your chosen technique, because all your opponent's energy will be spent in trying to maintain his balance.

PRINCIPLE 2: BODY GEOMETRY

DEFENSE: Your body will function with efficiency when you move it within its natural range of movements. When you try to move outside of these limits, you will discover that you are weak and are unable to transmit or resist power. All techniques are designed within these directional limits. Form and *kata* take you through a continuous sequence of movements within these limits, so that even in combat you are trained to be strong at all times.

ATTACK: Strategically, therefore, you should be trying to force your opponent into positions outside his limits. If you succeed, your opponent's structure will become weak and he will be unable to transmit or resist power. In fact, his energy will be spent in trying to keep his balance. Again, you will be delighted at the dramatic increase in the power of your technique.

PRINCIPLE 3: BREATH PARAMETERS

DEFENSE: If you breathe in or out too deeply, you will weaken your power considerably. Contrary to popular belief, your opponent should not be able to detect your breathing cycle. At the precise moment you feel your opponent is about to strike you, stop breathing for that instant, so that you can apply power whether you are breathing in or out. You should practice "pot bellied breathing" (i.e. pushing out your stomach as you breathe deeply), and breathing through the nose (flaring the nostrils) to stop your

opponent from detecting your breathing cycle. Keep your power in your stomach and always leave a third of the breath in the body. Pace your movement so that you don't change from "fight" to "flight" and weaken yourself.

ATTACK: Make your opponent alter his breathing pattern. You can do this, for example, by forcing him to move around and make him short of breath. When he has to open his mouth to breathe, when his shoulders start to heave, when his pallor changes and he has to use his chest to breathe, this is the time to attack strongly as his bodily state has visibly weakened. Also attack him as he breathes in.

PRINCIPLE 4: MENTAL FOCUS

DEFENSE: You must remain 100 percent mentally focused and not allow your mind to be distracted by anything else. This is probably the hardest principle to apply, but it is also the most powerful because it links all of the others. You must concentrate on the power drive from your feet, the power line through your stance, and the central power store in your abdomen maintained through your breathing. You must also always remain aware of your opponent. Your level of concentration will betray your level of skill.

ATTACK: Distract your opponent. Break his focus and attack him when he is unable to maintain his concentration. Watch for "dead" time when he becomes slothful or when his posture becomes dead through distraction. Attack his vital points when his concentration has lapsed.

MEDITATION IN MOTION

I call these principles 4 x 4 because each principle is inextricably linked to all the others. When one is broken, all the others are destroyed. Every true martial art is based on these four principles and they are essential to understanding why and how the various techniques work.

This is why we practice *karate ni sentenashi* (which means "there is no first attack in karate") as the *uke* (receiving) technique is designed to break the opponent's 4 x 4. Therefore our counter-attack is to a weakened opponent with an unstructured mind and body. Consequently we must always apply two techniques at once, usually utilizing both sides of the body, one side to receive and break the 4 x 4, and the other to transmit the energy back.

When you study the older techniques, forms and *kata*, you will discover these principles are applied consistently throughout them – and it will make sense of many of the apparently obscure movements. When you watch other martial arts, you will see how the same principles are applied to receive, lock, throw, sweep, trip, slip, strike and cut. By watching your opponents movements, you will also be able to judge their skill level.

In meditation, the same four principles are used. You maintain posture through balance; you maintain correct body alignment; you breathe correctly; and

you maintain proper mental focus and alertness in the same way as you do when you are training.

Sometimes students will approach their teacher and ask when they are going to be taught meditation. They go away somewhat confused when they are told that they have in fact been learning it for some time. Forms and *kata*, as stated previously, are like meditation in motion.

Ninety percent of martial arts skill
is in the mind. The purpose of
training is to develop a sharp,
responsive mind, unhindered by any
negative thoughts or emotions. A sharp
mind can organize what you have been
taught in an orderly fashion.

Your aim is
to therefore
achieve a peaceful and still mind that is,
nevertheless, deep and sharp.

Try practicing repetitive movements,
concentrating on good physical posture
and proper breathing. Having a peaceful
and still mind makes you a bit like the
"eye of a tornado": all around you is
action while your thoughts remain
focused and calm.

IT'S ALL IN THE MIND

POWER SITTING: A SIMPLE GUIDE TO MEDITATION

Meditation for many aspiring martial artists remains a mystery. Often their instructor will pay it lip service with a short period of "sitting" at the beginning and end of a lesson, but little other instruction is given. This brief guide will, hopefully, start to help you understand the basics and benefits of meditation. All good martial arts training is essentially meditation in motion, and this guide is designed to help you meditate when sitting or moving.

TIME

The reason for "sitting" just before practice is to help you to focus your mind on training, clearing all distractions, then relaxing your body before you begin. It is also good to "sit" after training, as this aids deep relaxation of the muscles and sharpens the mind allowing you to remember the lesson better. To get the most from meditation, you need to set aside a regular time that is free from distractions. The beginning and end of the day are often best, but you need to find a time that suits you.

You cannot watch the clock and meditate, so it is advisable to set an alarm clock for your allocated meditation time and turn it to face away from you.

At first you may find it strange to be in a "timeless zone" but it is important not to be governed by time.

So remember – do not look at the clock however much you may want to!

LOCATION

If possible, choose a place that is spacious and airy, as a good environment will aid the meditative process. The development of a calm mind is aided by a feeling of security, and if you can't feel settled then it is difficult to apply yourself. You lose your concentration and tend to daydream.

The more that you meditate in '"your place," the more stable and settled you will feel. Inside the training hall is a perfectly good location. For everyday meditation, use the room that you always train in at home. Meditating outdoors in a natural environment is also very relaxing. Playing atmospheric music can also help to induce a deep feeling of peace.

POSTURE

Your knees need to be at least as high as your hips. To achieve this, sit cross-legged, either on a kitchen chair or on the floor. If you sit on the floor, support your buttocks with a cushion or meditation stool. Sitting in the '"lotus position" (sitting cross-legged with your feet resting on top of the opposite thighs) requires no other support, but many Westerners find this position uncomfortable and give up because of the pain it causes in their knees. If my joints are stiff from training, I sit on a kitchen chair where the back rest gives my back some support. Otherwise, I use a firm cushion on the floor, or pillows from the bed if I am traveling and staying in a hotel.

Maintain an upright posture. If you slump it will cause discomfort, so try to imagine that you are being drawn upwards from the top of your head. The small of your back should have a natural, unforced curve which feels comfortable to you.

You should feel that you are being gently pushed between the shoulder blades. Gently release any tension in your neck and shoulders by shrugging them and moving them backwards and forwards. Keep your knees in line with your hips, and hold your arms lightly against your stomach. Make sure that you are working with your body and not against it.

BREATHING

Breathing is like a stick of bamboo. A bamboo stick has straight sections and, every so often along its length, a knot. Breathing in and out is like the straight part of the bamboo, and the points between an inhale and exhale are the knots.

Inhale from your *tanden* (a point in the center of your body between your navel and groin). Focus your breath down with a silent *kiai* (a spirit shout) and then allow it to escape gently, at a natural pace, through your nose. Just at the point where you would have to stop yourself from exhaling, begin the process again until, like the bamboo, your breathing pattern is an unbroken line. Breathing should be steady and relaxing. You should allow your mind to follow the sensation of the breath and its rhythm.

ATTENTIVENESS

You are not trying to go into a trance, only to sharpen the workings of your mind – so when your mind is distracted, simply bring it back. By gathering your attention and focusing it on the breath, you will develop patience and understanding. This is a goal that everyone, with a little perseverance, can achieve.

EYES

Keep your eyes open and keep your attention focused on the farthest edges of your field of vision. This allows you to see everything at once rather than one thing at a time.

AWARENESS

If you feel drowsy, pay attention to your posture. Remember the following rule: every time your mind wanders, your awareness drops and your posture slumps. Do not feel disappointed – simply continue. If you feel disappointed because you are not as successful as you want to be, simply note these feelings and continue.

Allow your awareness to spread through your body, letting go of excess tension wherever you find it.

This is only a simple guide to get you started. The aim is to help you enjoy the feeling that comes from understanding how martial arts training is a form of meditation. The nature of movement within both mind and body cannot be understood without understanding stillness first. And the joy of stillness cannot be understood without experiencing movement in contrast. One naturally reflects the other.

One of the founding fathers of modern karate, Gichin Funakoshi, stated that there is no first attack in karate. All true martial arts techniques begin with a "receiving" movement, thus returning the opponent's force. This enables the martial artist to remain nonaggressive.

There are four basic receiving moves common to most of the martial arts. They are:

- ☯ The rising head block
- ☯ The inner to outer middle block
- ☯ The outer to inner middle block
- ☯ The low sweeping block.

The moves used by beginners for blocking an attack will shortly have an even greater significance. For the more experienced practitioners these same moves become locks, throws and strikes to vital points of the body.

Imagine the effect that these moves have on an aggressor. The attacker is essentially trying to hit a spinning ball. At the moment of impact, the defender's arm is rotating and traveling in a similar direction to the attacker's. This changes the direction of the attackers thrust, pulling him off balance.

SELF-DEFENSE

THE FIST

The fist is one of the martial artist's most important weapons. The ideal martial arts fist is as follows:

The fingers should be closed in and squeezed tight. Always pay particular attention to the two fingers furthest away from the thumb. These two fingers work the major muscle group in the forearm and improve the grip, making the wrist strong. Flex the fist to get the two striking knuckles to protrude.

The thumb should wrap around and go underneath the index finger, pulling it backward to help tighten the fist. There now should be a straight line from the top of the arm to the wrist and hand so the line of power extends from the shoulder through to the first two knuckles.

KICKS

There are four basic kicks:

- ☯ The front kick
- ☯ The side kick
- ☯ The back kick
- ☯ The round kick
  (see page 74).

Every other kick is a variation on one of the above.

If you take one long step forward, then you can kick in any direction to your own head height. Once you combine this ability with the basic principles of punching, you can use your whole body to create power beyond your wildest dreams!

NATURAL MOVEMENT

When we talk about "natural movement" in the martial arts, we are referring to natural and fluid movement of the body. It is easy for the mind to concentrate too hard on the movement, creating excessive tension and muscle stiffness. This is the most common cause of slow, powerless kicks. If you try "meditation in motion" your kicks should become much smoother and more powerful.

The hips are constructed in such a way to allow free movement forwards and backwards (to let you walk), with a small degree of movement to the side. All kicks can be done using this alignment, changing the angle of the body to fit the target and rotating the upper body against the lower. Karate *kata* is structured to give you the necessary flexibility and accompanying strength to be able to do all of these kicks to head height.

It is no use trying to make your body do things it was never intended to do.

Many people stretch and tear the soft tissue around the joints in their efforts to allow movement beyond their natural alignment. Joint damage will result from such movement, because force normally absorbed by the soft tissue is then put directly on the joint in its weakened, unprotected position.

EXERCISES

The following exercises concentrate on natural movement and joint alignment.

1 Stand sideways with one arm and shoulder resting lightly against a wall to help you balance. Swing the leg furthest from the wall forwards and upwards, allowing a small natural bend at the knee joint. Aim the leg towards an imaginary target directly in front of you. Increase the height gradually as you feel more comfortable. You will discover that after a few swings you can easily reach head height. This gives you the flexibility and alignment needed for the front kick.

2 Now turn forty five degrees to the imaginary target and repeat the process. This is known as the half-hip-twist roundhouse kick. Your supporting foot should be at a right angle to the target, and you can allow your upper torso to counter-rotate so that you can counter-balance the movement.

3 Now stand facing the wall and lean forward about forty-five degrees. Place your hands on the wall and swing your leg easily up backwards. Gradually increase the height of the swing until you cannot get your leg any higher. This is your back kick. If you twist your upper body so that your arm runs down the back of your kicking leg, it becomes the side kick. If you alter the foot positioning to point the foot and toes, it becomes the full-hip-twist version of the roundhouse kick described in 2. You'll be familiar with them all in time!

SUPPORTING FOOT

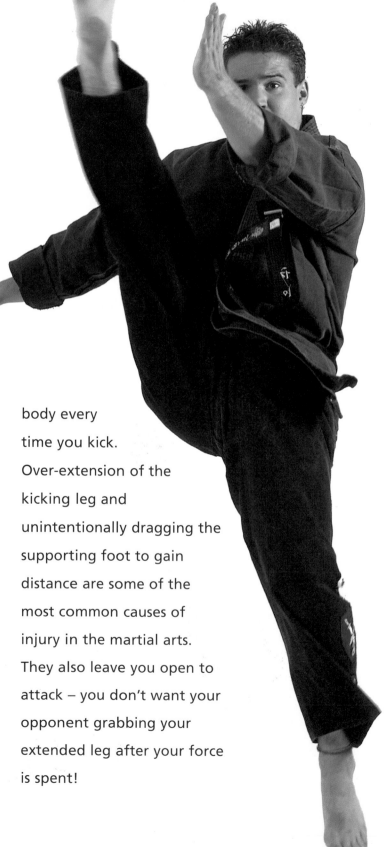

In all martial arts movements, the placing of the feet is of vital importance because this placement dictates the power lines through the body. The angle of the supporting foot will dictate the angle of transmission of power through the kicking leg in the same way that it dictates the angle and distance of the body to the target.

Remember that for every force going in one direction, there is an equal force going in the opposite direction. To give your kick the required power, you must push down with your supporting foot in the opposite direction to the kick. Practice continually, changing the distances and angles to your target so that you instinctively take the correct position with your body every time you kick. Over-extension of the kicking leg and unintentionally dragging the supporting foot to gain distance are some of the most common causes of injury in the martial arts. They also leave you open to attack – you don't want your opponent grabbing your extended leg after your force is spent!

Your center of balance is located at the *tanden,* the point in your body between your navel and groin. To inject your body weight into a kick, you must ensure that your center of balance moves with you and is powering your leg at the moment of impact. A good martial artist has a subconscious awareness of this point in his or her body.

CENTER OF
BALANCE

USE OF HIPS

The hips move not just on one axis but on three.

1 They tip forwards and backwards (used in front and back kicks).

2 They rotate horizontally to the body (used in round-house kicks and when doing any kick from the back leg).

3 They tip (or wiggle) from side to side (used to obtain movement in roundhouse and sidekicks).

The hips are "fired" by the counter-force from the supporting foot to the center of balance. They then "vibrate" on the required axis in order to inject and withdraw the power from the target and to give focus to the kick.

CENTERLINE

The object is to "hit" the centerline of your opponent. Draw an imaginary line through the center of your opponent's body – whatever angle you kick at, you should strike this line. This will give you the correct penetration and focus to drop your opponent. If you strike to the front of the body, the kick will be weak. If you aim through the body, it will be a push and lack focus.

So, when placing the supporting foot for distance and angle, the correct target must be accounted for.

KNEE POSITION

It is vital to hit the target in as straight a line as possible, in order to maximize the effect of the kick and to make it more difficult for the opponent to block. The best way to ensure this is to raise the knee as high as possible by pulling it into your chest before you release the lower part of the leg. This action has several other beneficial effects: It ensures a vigorous use of the hamstring to prevent the foot from swinging outwards at the beginning of the movement and brings the foot in front of the hips so that it can be "driven" by your center of balance.

This also makes it much more difficult to over-extend the knee joint and prevents the foot from "arcing" upwards. In the front, roundhouse and side kicks, you bring the knee into the chest, and in the back kick you bring the chest down to the knee – but the angle between the knee and body is always the same.

TO RE-CAP

1 Good *kata* (see page 34) provides you with the correct warm up, flexibility and strength required for kicking.

2 Move naturally and easily. Utilize the momentum gained from the movement to help power the kick.

3 Push in the opposite direction to the kick through the supporting foot to the ground.

4 Use your center of balance to put your weight into the kick.

5 Rotate the hips on the necessary axis to obtain penetration and focus.

6 Distance and angle to the target is determined by the positioning of the supporting foot. For instance, if your supporting foot is too far away from your opponent, you simply will not be able to reach them.

7 Strike the centerline of the opponent's body and in as straight a line as possible for maximum effect.

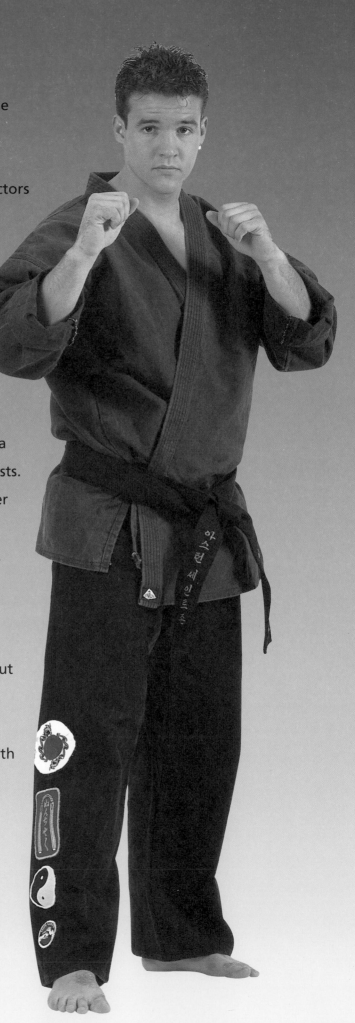

Acrobatics and the martial arts originally came together in the Chinese Opera. As a result of their popularity in recent times, the kung-fu movie craze was born and actors began performing some of the most amazing physical routines possible.

One of these stars, Bruce Lee, brought the craze to the West with his dazzling film *Enter The Dragon*, which is now a cult classic. His jumping, spinning kicks and on-screen charisma were an inspiration to all martial artists.

Lee was followed by a host of other martial arts actors, including Jackie Chan, Steven Segal and Chuck Norris. Then, of course, came the Power Rangers!

As human beings, we are naturally dextrous with our hands and arms, but less so with our legs and feet. Therefore we have to train much harder to be precise when kicking with our feet – particularly when we are flying through the air!

On the following pages I perform and explain some of my most astonishing kicks.

FLYING SIDE KICK

This is the most spectacular martial arts technique of all. Tradition tells us that it was devised to knock opponents off horseback and, when you see it in action, you can believe it!

Although the end result is always the same mid-air position, the kick can start in three different ways:

- Leaping into the air from a standing position
- Running and leaping
- Jumping from another object

In every case, you perform a side kick while in the air – just like we have seen in the movies. In fact, it's a technique made famous by screen hero and martial arts expert Bruce Lee.

But don't think that because you have seen it so often that the flying side kick is easy! My background is in tae kwon do, a martial art famous for its flying kicks. I have practiced for many years to perform this kick, so please

don't try it without first undergoing years of proper training.

SPINNING HOOK KICK

The spinning hook kick is a dazzling and dizzying movement!

The technique involves spinning 360 degrees to kick an opponent with the rear of the leg before finishing back in the starting position.

It catches the opponent by surprise as it comes round outside his line of vision and often hits him from behind.

The spinning hook kick requires a great deal of body control, particularly when spinning, to get the right directional force and focus.

Notice how I look over my shoulder before kicking, in order to target the move correctly. Also note how I pull around by turning on the supporting foot and bending the kicking leg. This makes the point of impact precisely on the returning arc of the foot.

This kick often follows a hand technique or a front,

round or side kick. It is usually used at the end of a display and makes for a great movie technique because it is visually dramatic. This kick was made particularly famous by Chuck Norris, another Korean stylist and martial arts star.

Be warned – this technique requires a good degree of flexibility, agility and technical skill. Sometimes you can practice by repeating the same kick again and again in sequence… but watch that you don't get giddy!

ROUND KICK FOLLOWED BY JUMPING CRESCENT KICK

This is brilliant because both kicks are performed off the same leg! The round kick continues to go round and confuses the opponent. Then, just as he thinks that your back is exposed to him, you jump into the air, making a 180 degree turn – and hit him with a crescent kick with the same leg!

1

2

3

Jab, Spinning Backfist and Reverse Punch

1

Starting from the open-hand back stance, step up and jab with the front hand. Notice how I sneak up with the back foot, gaining ground without the opponent realizing. I then spin around with the backfist, continuing the turn to finish off with a devastating reverse punch. Return to the open-hand back stance.

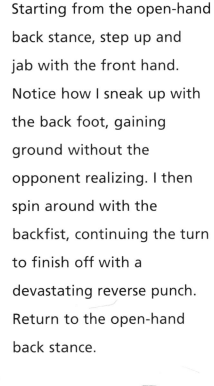

2

3

4

CONCLUSION

I hope you have enjoyed reading this book as much as I enjoyed working on it.

The martial arts are an excellent way of improving the quality of your life if you observe the ground rules.

You will form friendships for life – grounded in shared sweat and effort. You will also travel to places to train and compete that you would not otherwise visit.

Look after your mind, body, animals, friends, family, and the environment and they will take care of you.

Only then will you understand the true meaning of the martial arts.

COMMON TERMS

ETIQUETTE, COMMANDS AND PHRASES USED AT THE DOJO

DOJO: Training hall or any place of training; literally 'do' is 'the way' and 'jo' is 'the place'

GAKUSAI: Student

GI: Training suit

HANSHI: A person who one should copy or emulate

KARATEKA: Student of karate

KOHAI: One's junior

OBI: Belt

SEMPAI: One's senior

SENSEI: Instructor; literally 'One who has been before'

DOMO: Thanks (informal)

DOMO ARIGATO GOZIAMASU: Thank you very much (formal)

DOZO: Please excuse me

EMBERCEN: The class is starting, please line up

HAI: Yes, or acknowledgement of understanding

HAJIME: Begin

KIRITSU: Stand up into the ready stance

MAWATTE: Turn around

MOKUSO: Meditation

MUKOSO YAMAE: Finish meditation

NOREI: Prepare to bow

OTAGAI NI REI: Class bows to the Dojo and to those assembled

REI: Bow

SEIZA: Kneel down

SENSEI NI REI: Class bowing to the instructor and the instructor bowing to class

SONABADE IPPON TORU: Perform single punch without step

YAMAE: Finish and return to ready stance

YO-OI: Ready stance

ANATOMICAL

ASHI: Foot

ASHI KUBI: Ankle

CHUDAN: Middle region of body

GAMEN: Chin, jaw

GEDAN: Lower region of body

HARA: Abdomen

HIJI: Elbow

HIZA: Knee

JODAN: Upper region of body

KAKATO: Heel

NAKASUMI: Center line of body

SHAMEN: Side of head

SUI GETSU: Solar plexus

SUNDEN: Between eyes

SUNE: Shin

TE: Hand

TE KUBI: Wrist

TE NO UCHI: Palm

COMPETITION TERMINOLOGY

AIUCHI: Simultaneous strikes

AKA IPPON: Red scores one point

AKA NO KACHI: Red wins

AKA WAZA-ARI: Red scores half point

ATOSHI BARAKU: More time left

DAISHOSEN: Deciding bout

ENCHO SEN: Extended bout

FUJUBUN: Technique insufficient

FUKUSHIN: Judge

FUSENSHO-O: Bye

HANSOKU: Foul

HANSOKU-CHUI: Ippon penalty

HANTEI: Decision

HIKIWAKE: Draw or tie

JOGAI: Exit from fighting area

JOGAI-CHUI: Ippon penalty for leaving fighting area

KANSA: Arbitrator

KEIKOKU: Waza-ari penalty

KIKEN: Withdrawal

MOTONO ICHI: Resume original position

MUBOBI: No guard or no respect for own safety

SHIKKAKU: Disqualification

SHIRO IPPON: White scores one point

SHIRO NO KACHI: White wins

SHIRO WAZA-ARI: White scores half point

SHOBU HAJIME: Start the extended match

SHOBU IPPON HAJIME: Start 1 point match

SHOBU SANBON – HAJIME: Start 3 point match

SHUGO: Judge called

SHUSHIN: Referee

SONEMADE: End of match

TORIMASEN: No scoring technique

TSUZUKETE: Continue fight

TSUZUKETE HAJIME: Start fight

YAME: Stop

KATA

Collection of variable training principles, strategies and techniques constructed into a ritual training pattern

STANCES

FUDO DACHI: Low drop stance

GYAKUZUKI DACHI: Name given to Zenkutsudachi stance when performing a Gyakuzuki punch

GYAKU NEKOASHI DACHI: Reverse cat stance

HACHIJI DACHI: Figure-eight stance, named after its resemblance to the Japanese letter for eight

HEISOKU DACHI: Closed toes stance

JIGO TAI: Normal standing stance

JUNZUKI DACHI: Name given to Zenkutsudachi stance when performing a Junzuki punch

KIBA DACHI: Outer circular stance, feet pointing forwards

KOKUTSU DACHI: Back stance

KOSA DACHI: Cross stance

MUSUBI DACHI: Attention stance, feet forming a V

NAIHANCHI: Inner circular stance

NEKOASHI HANMI: Half facing cat stance

NEKOASHI MAHANMI: Side facing cat stance

NEKOASHI SHOMEN: Front facing cat stance

NOTSUKKOMI DACHI: Stance used to perform longer deeper techniques than can be used with Zenkutsudachi

SAGI-ASH DACHI: Heron stance, one legged stance

SHIKO DACHI: Outer circular stance, feet pointing out

SHIZENTAI: Normal ready stance with one foot in front

TATE SEISHAN: Vertical stance with toes of front foot in-line with heel of back foot

YOKO SEISHAN: Sideward stance with heel of front foot in-line with toes of back foot

ZENKUTSUDACHI: Front stance: general name given to stances where the majority of the weight is on the front leg

PUNCHING

FURI ZUKI: Hook punch
GYAKUZUKI: Reverse punch
JUNZUKI: Lung punch
MOROTE-ZUKI: Double fist punch
NAGASHIZUKI: Slipping punch
TOBIGYAKUZUKI: Reverse hand jab
TOBIKOMI ZUKI: Leading hand jab

FOOT & LEG STRIKES

FUMIKOMI: Stamping kick
HIZA GERI: Knee kick
KAKATO GERI: Heel kick, axe kick
MAE GERI: Front kick
MAWASHI GERI: Round house kick
MIKA ZUKI GERI: Crescent kick
NIDAN GERI: Double jump kick
SOKUTO GERI: Blade of foot kick
USHIRO GERI: Back kick
USHIRO MAWASHI GERI: Reverse round house kick
YOKO GERI: Side kick

HAND STRIKES

EMPI (HIJI) UCHI: Elbow strike
HAISHO UCHI: Back of hand strike
HAITO UCHI: Ridge hand strike
HIRAKEN UCHI: Flat fist strike
KEIKO UCHI: Beak fist strike
KOKEN UCHI: Arch fist strike
NUKITE UCHI: Spear hand strike
SHUTO UCHI: Open hand strike
TEISHO UCHI: Palm heel strike
TETTSUI UCHI: Hammer fist strike
URAKEN UCHI: Back fist strike

HAND SHAPES

HAITO: Ridge hand
HITOSASHI IPPONKEN: First finger single knuckle fist

IPPON NUKITE: One finger strike
IPPONKEN: Single knuckle fist
KEIKO: Beak hand
KOKO: Tiger mouth hand
NAKADAKA IPPONKEN: Middle finger single knuckle fist
NIHON NUKITE: Two finger strike
NUKITE: Spear hand
OYOYUBI IPPONKEN: Thumb knuckle single knuckle fist
SEIKEN: Normal fist
SHUTO: Open hand
TEISHO: Palm heel
TETTSUI: Bottom fist or hammer fist
URAKEN: Back fist

FOOT SHAPES FOR STRIKING

JOSOKUTO: Ball of foot
YUBISAKI: Toes
SOKUTO: Open foot, using the outside edge of the foot
HAISOKU: Instep
CHUSOKU: Sole of foot
KAKTO: Heel of foot

UKE (receiving or blocking techniques)

ATOSHI UKE: Downward block
BON SAU: Wing arm block (Chinese naming)
GEDAN UKE (BARAI): Lower block
HAITO UKE: Ridge hand block
JODAN UKE: Upper block
JUJI UKE: Crossed arm block
KAKATE UKE: Hooking hand block
MOROTE UKE: Double handed block
NAGASHI UKE: Slipping, brushing or evading block
SHUTO UKE: Open hand block
SOTO UKE: Outer block
SUKUI UKE: Scooping block
TEISHO UKE: Palm Heel block
UCHI UKE: Inner block

DIRECTIONAL & POSITIONAL

MAE: Front
USHIRO (URE): Back (Reverse)
MIGI: Right
YOKO: Side
SURIKOMI: Step up with back foot to front foot
HIDARI: Left
AIHANMI: Same side forward as opponent (both in left stance for example)

GYAKUHANMI: Opposite side forward as opponent

NUMERIC

(Cardinal numbers, as used for counting)
(Dan Grades & Kata)
(Ordinal numbers, as adjectives — 'first', 'second' etc)
1: Ichi, Shodan, Ipponme
2: Ni, Nidan, Nihonme
3: Sun, Sandan, Sanbonme
4: Shi, Yondan, Yonhonme
5: Go, Godan, Gohonme
6: Roku, Rokudan, Ropponme
7: Shichi, Shichidan, Nanahonme
8: Hachi, Hachidan, Hachihonme
9: Ku, Kudan, Kyuhonme
10: Ju, Judan, Jipponme

COMMONLY USED WORDS & SAYINGS

HEI JO SHIN: Keep your usual mind
IN-YO: Japanese name for Yin-Yang
KARATE NI SENTINASHI: There is no first attack in karate
KIAI: 'Harmony of spirit', generally the term used for the sound made at particular points in technique when the Kime is expressed orally
KIME: The focus that exists in a technique
METSUKE: Perception, sight
METSUKE NO EZAN: 'Gazing at the distant mountains', describing the type of sight used where the eyes focus at a distance, but see everything
MUSHIN: 'Void mind'
SHO SHIN: Beginners mind
YIN-YANG: The symbol of opposites and balance
ZANSHIN: Awareness, mindfulness of surrounding and situations, presence, attention, concentration, remaining prepared
YAKUSOKU: Prearranged
KIHON: Basic
KUMITE: Sparring
TAISABAKI: Body Skill
KAWASHI: Avoiding
NOGARE: Escaping
NAGASHI: Sweep away
IRIMI: Entering

CREDITS

Co-author Steve Rowe – 6th dan karate, 3rd dan iaido – is seen here on the right with Austin and 4th dan karateka, John Wright (on left).

Steve has been an exponent of the martial arts for more than twenty-five years. He is the founder of Shi Kon Budokai with over 16,000 students and a further worldwide membership. Steve writes two columns a month in *Traditional Karate* magazine, which is the most popular English language karate magazine in the world.